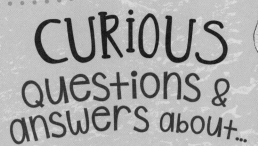

CURIOUS Questions & answers about...

Astronauts

What's the one special OBJECT you'd take into space with you?

How TALL are you?

What unique SKILL do you have that would make you a great astronaut?

Would you rather float about in space or speed around with a space pack?

What's the longest JOURNEY you've ever been on?

Words by Sue Becklake

Illustrations by Pauline Reeves

MILES KELLY

What is an astronaut?

An astronaut is a specially trained person who leaves Earth to travel into space. All around Earth, space stretches out between the distant planets and stars.

Moon

Astronauts are in here!

Rocket

Why do astronauts go into space?

To explore different places, such as the Moon, and to find out what it is like to live in space.

I am a cosmonaut, the Russian name for an astronaut.

How long do they spend in space?

Astronauts usually stay on the International Space Station (ISS) for six months, but four astronauts have spent over a year in space.

5

How do astronauts get into space?

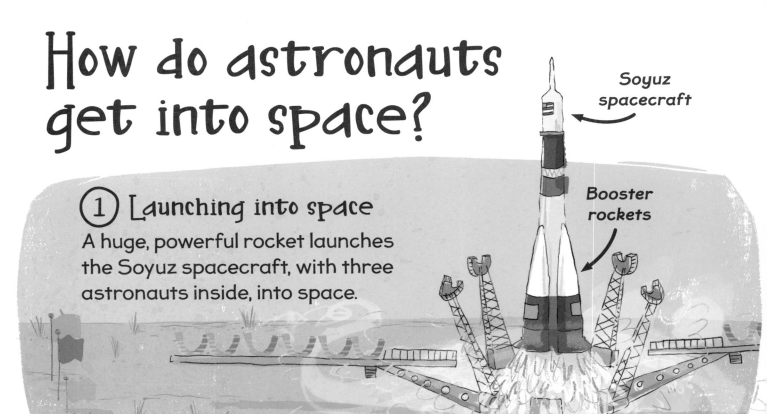

Soyuz spacecraft

① Launching into space

A huge, powerful rocket launches the Soyuz spacecraft, with three astronauts inside, into space.

Booster rockets

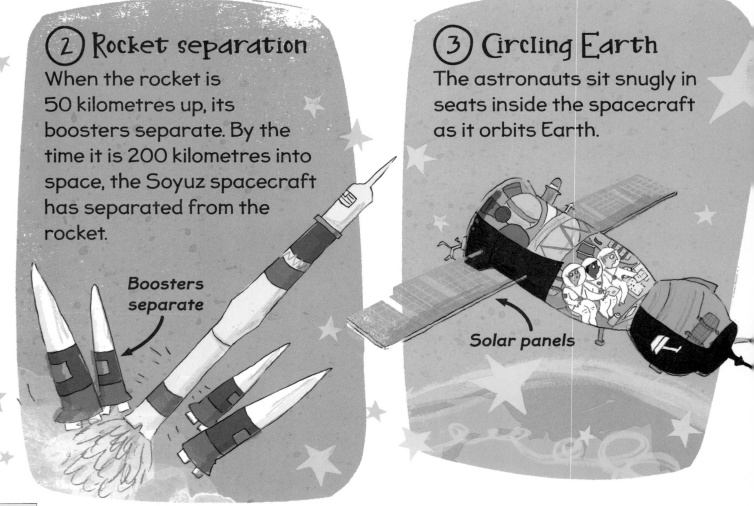

② Rocket separation

When the rocket is 50 kilometres up, its boosters separate. By the time it is 200 kilometres into space, the Soyuz spacecraft has separated from the rocket.

Boosters separate

③ Circling Earth

The astronauts sit snugly in seats inside the spacecraft as it orbits Earth.

Solar panels

④ Docking

The spacecraft catches up with the ISS and locks onto it. The astronauts can then climb on board to meet the ISS crew.

ISS docking port

⑤ Heading home

When the Soyuz spacecraft re-enters the air around Earth it is going extremely fast. The outside rubs against the air and gets incredibly hot, but the astronauts are safe inside. It's a bumpy ride though!

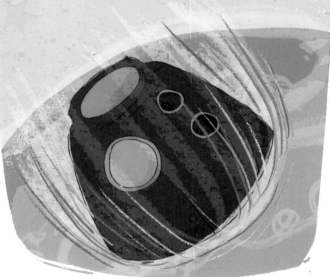

⑥ Safe landing

Astronauts feel nothing more than a bump when they land on the ground. They are helped onto recliners because their legs are weak after months of living in space.

Can anyone be an astronaut?

Any adult person who is fit and healthy can travel in space. Astronauts who go to the ISS have months of training, but in the future ordinary people will be able to go to space.

How do astronauts get used to floating in space?

In a big aeroplane flying in loops, trainee astronauts float for a short time as though they were weightless.

Now i know why they call this big plane the Vomit Comet – it makes me feel sick.

How do trainees practise spacewalks?

Wearing spacesuits underwater, they float in a huge tank. They can practise everything they will do when they go on spacewalks.

Vomit Comet

Aspiring astronauts need to be very healthy because there are no hospitals in space. They also need to know about science or engineering.

What special skills do they need?

Astronauts have to learn how everything on the space station works and how to fix it if it goes wrong. They also practise doing the experiments planned for their space trip.

Neutral Buoyancy Laboratory (underwater)

Did you know?

Astronauts built the **ISS**, joining the parts together in space.

Russian cosmonaut, Yuri Gagarin, was the **first person** to fly into space on 10 April 1961.

Between 1981 and 2011, American **space shuttles** carried astronauts into space. The shuttles flew many times, taking off like a rocket and landing back on a runway like a plane.

Spacewalking astronauts use a **tether** to fix themselves to the ISS so they can't float off.

You can sometimes see the ISS moving slowly across the sky like a **bright star** just after sunset.

Astronauts add **liquid** salt and pepper to their food. Grains or powder would float around and get into vital equipment.

The first person to walk on the **Moon** in July 1969 was Neil Armstrong.

Many astronauts get **space sick**, like travel sickness, but it soon wears off.

The first female astronaut, and the only **woman** to fly solo in space, was Valentina Tereshkova in 1963.

Peggy Whitson was the first **female commander** of the ISS in 2007 and 2016.

There have been **seven** astronaut tourists who have paid millions of dollars to fly to the ISS.

What do astronauts wear?

Inside a space station they wear ordinary clothes, but outside astronauts need a spacesuit to keep them alive. Spacesuits are very expensive – each costs about $12 million.

A backpack, called a Life Support System, carries oxygen to breathe and water for cooling

The helmet's gold visor protects the astronaut's eyes from the strong sunlight

I can talk to the rest of the crew using the microphone and earphones in my cap.

Astronauts sip drinking water through a tube near their mouth

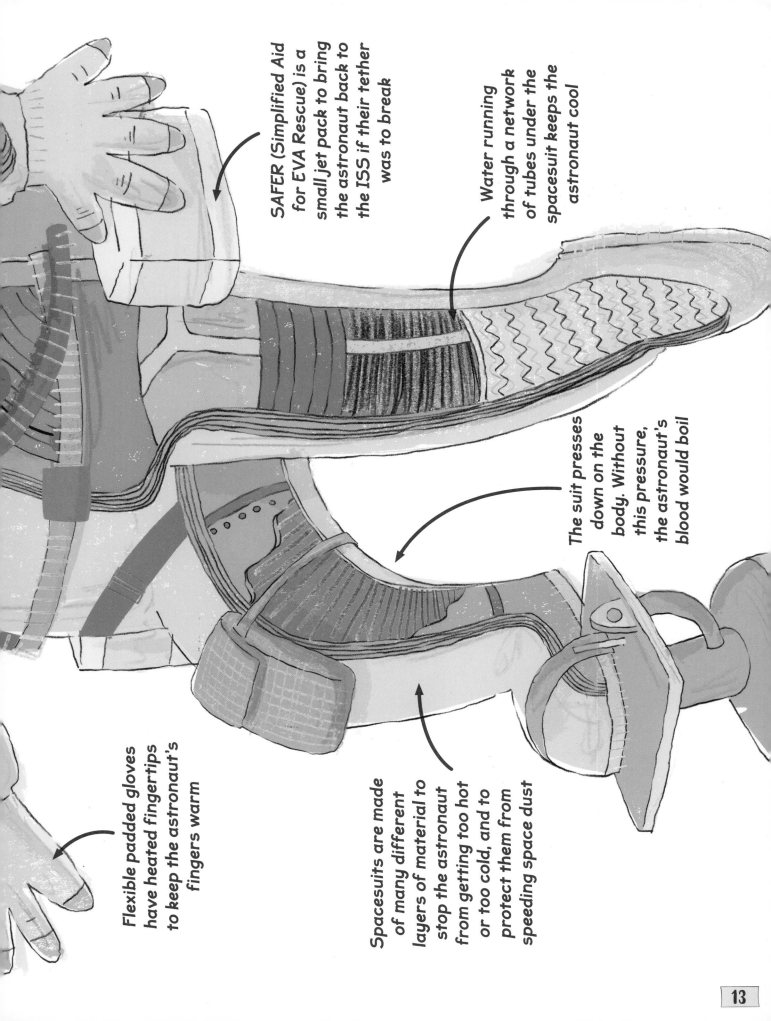

SAFER (Simplified Aid for EVA Rescue) is a small jet pack to bring the astronaut back to the ISS if their tether was to break

Water running through a network of tubes under the spacesuit keeps the astronaut cool

The suit presses down on the body. Without this pressure, the astronaut's blood would boil

Flexible padded gloves have heated fingertips to keep the astronaut's fingers warm

Spacesuits are made of many different layers of material to stop the astronaut from getting too hot or too cold, and to protect them from speeding space dust

Where do astronauts live?

The International Space Station, which is circling the Earth, is home to astronauts exploring space. It is made of sections called modules where astronauts can eat, sleep and work.

Does everything float in a space station?

Yes! On Earth, gravity pulls everything down to the ground, but in a space station, the astronauts and everything else like food, water and tools float around if they are not fixed down. We say they are weightless.

Docking area

International Space Station

How do astronauts get food and water?

Everything they need is delivered from Earth in a Soyuz spacecraft or a robot ferry.

Is it easy to sleep in space?

Not really! Astronauts fix their sleeping bag to the wall so they don't float around and bump into things while they are asleep.

Sleeping area

I wear earplugs and an eye mask to keep out the noise and light so I can sleep.

Living and sleeping area

Solar panels

Laboratory area

Where does the electricity come from?

Huge solar panels on the space station turn sunlight into electricity to run all the equipment.

Solar panels

15

How many?

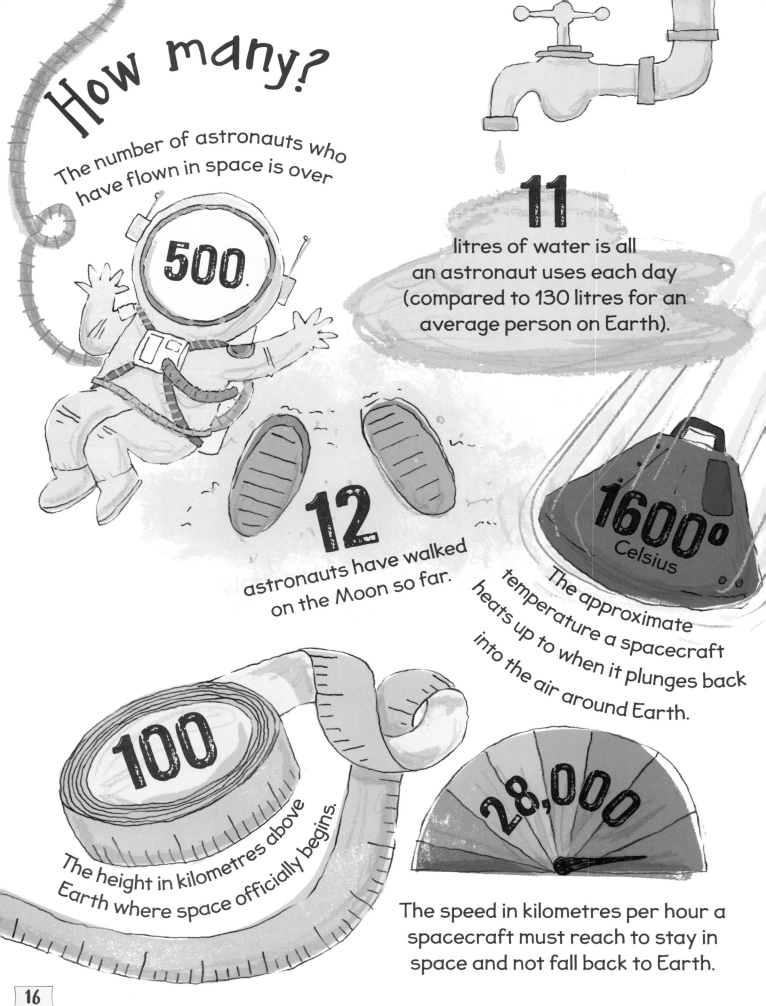

The number of astronauts who have flown in space is over **500**.

11 litres of water is all an astronaut uses each day (compared to 130 litres for an average person on Earth).

12 astronauts have walked on the Moon so far.

1600° Celsius The approximate temperature a spacecraft heats up to when it plunges back into the air around Earth.

100 The height in kilometres above Earth where space officially begins.

28,000 The speed in kilometres per hour a spacecraft must reach to stay in space and not fall back to Earth.

The ISS has a supply of about **2400** litres of water but over 90 percent of it, including toilet water and sweat, is recycled!

Astronauts from **18** different countries have lived on the ISS.

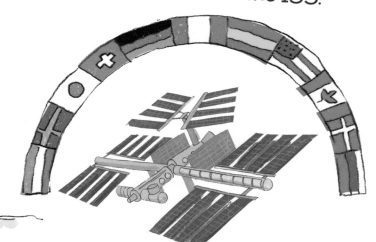

The oldest astronaut so far is John Glenn. He went into space at the age of **77**.

3 The number of days it took the Apollo astronauts to get to the Moon.

A spacesuit backpack provides an astronaut with about **8.5** hours of oxygen and water, and enough nitrogen gas for the SAFER jet thrusters to power back to the ISS.

What do astronauts eat?

They eat the same as you, but choose their favourite foods before they go. The food is cooked on Earth and then sent to the space station in ready-to-eat portions.

Food is dried so it lasts longer and is lighter for the journey.

Adding hot water to this packet of dried food makes it into a tasty meal. The packet is fixed to my tray to stop it floating away.

Spaghetti

Cups are no good to us, because drinks float out of them. We add water to a packet of dried powder then suck the drink through a straw.

19

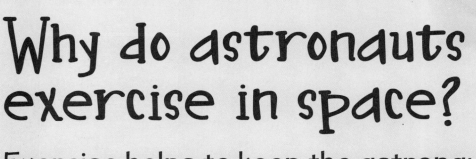

Why do astronauts exercise in space?

Exercise helps to keep the astronauts strong and healthy. Their bodies change in space without gravity to pull them down to the ground. They get taller, and their bones and muscles get weaker.

How much exercise do they do?

Two hours of exercise every day is enough to keep an astronaut's heart and muscles strong.

My space exercise bike doesn't have a saddle. A harness keeps me in place and my feet clip onto the pedals.

What jobs are done in space?

Astronauts are very busy. They look after the ISS, keep it clean and tidy, and repair anything that goes wrong. They also do lots of experiments.

> We monitor our bodies to see how we cope with weightlessness.

Who cleans the ISS?

Everyone helps to clean once a week. Astronauts use a vacuum cleaner to remove dust. They also check everything is working well and fix it if not.

> I'm using wipes and a cloth sprayed with detergent to remove any dirt.

> One day we may be able to grow most of our own food in space.

What experiments do astronauts do?

They try to find out how things, such as crystals and plants, grow differently in space.

What is an EVA?

Extravehicular Activity (EVA) is the name for a spacewalk. This is when astronauts put on spacesuits to work outside the space station, installing new equipment or doing repairs.

Do astronauts have robot helpers?

Yes! Canadarm2 is a robot arm on the outside of the ISS. Astronauts operate it from inside, and it can help to move or install bulky parts.

Why do astronauts take living things into space?

They study how things behave differently in space. They grow seeds, as well as watch insects and small animals to study how quickly they get used to weightlessness.

Would you rather?

Eeuww, stinky smells! Would you rather live in the **sealed** ISS or on Earth where you can just **open** a window?

Would you rather **live** in a space station circling Earth or **travel** for six months to visit Mars?

Time for pooping practice! Would you prefer a **comfy toilet** at home or aiming at a teeny hole on a **space toilet**?

If you were working in space, would you prefer to **suit up** for a space walk outside or stay inside in **pyjamas** to operate a robot arm?

Would you rather watch spiders **spin webs** or ants **build tunnels** in weightlessness?

Would you prefer to float inside a **space station** or float around a **swimming pool** on Earth?

Would you rather play **golf** on the Moon (like astronaut Alan Shephard in 1971) or **table tennis** on the ISS?

Would you prefer to look down at **Earth** from the ISS or stare at the **Moon** from Earth through a telescope?

Can astronauts take a bath?

Astronauts don't bath in space, because water would not run out of a tap or stay in a bath. Water turns into balls of liquid that float around.

To wash my hair I rub shampoo and a little water into it, then use a comb and towel to remove the dirt.

Instead of taking a shower, I have washed myself with a soapy cloth and am now towelling dry.

How about having a shower instead?

The US Skylab space station in 1973 did have a shower. It was sealed shut to keep all the water inside and the astronauts had to vacuum up the water before they could get out.

How do they brush their teeth?

> I clean my teeth with an ordinary toothbrush, but use special toothpaste that I can swallow. There's no need to rinse with water.

Do astronauts do laundry?

Astronauts save water by not washing their clothes. They throw away their underwear and socks, but keep wearing the same outer clothes for about six weeks!

Space toilet

Where does their poo go?

Space toilets do not use water for flushing. Flowing air sucks the waste away into bags to be recycled or taken back to Earth. Astronauts have to fix themselves down so they stay on the toilet.

Will people ever visit Mars?

Yes, there are plans to send people to Mars. The journey will take six months each way. They will have to take everything they need to stay alive — food, water and air to breathe.

Possible Mars colony

Command centre

What would people wear on Mars?

Laboratory

I'd need a spacesuit to provide air to breathe, and to keep warm and safe from radiation and blowing dust.

Is there any water to drink?

There is no running water on Mars, but there is frozen ice that could be used near its north and south poles.

Could people sunbathe on Mars?

It would be far too cold! Mars is further from the Sun than Earth. It's also dry and windy, and there are often huge dust storms.

Dust storm

Is the air on Mars breathable?

No. Humans need oxygen gas to breathe and the air on Mars is mostly carbon dioxide gas.

Wind energy generators

Radio communication building

Living pod

Where could they live?

If astronauts built homes on Mars, they would need thick walls to protect against dangerous radiation. They might even build homes underground.

Living pod

A compendium of questions

How often do astronauts see a sunrise?

They see the Sun rise and set 16 times every day from the ISS as it circles Earth.

How big is the ISS?

The living space inside is bigger than a six-bedroom house. The whole station stretches out to about the size of a sports field.

How many astronauts live on the ISS?

Usually six, but there are nine when a new crew arrives.

How fast does the ISS travel?

27,600 kilometres an hour, about 30 times faster than a Boeing 747 jet.